Wally
Yvette Hart

(April 2013 - Suffolk, VA
w/ Ian Clayton)

i

Other Books Coming in 2013
(Titles may change)

"An Introduction to Angels"

"The Spiritual Dynamics of Hand Drumming"

"Engaging: Adventuring on the Other side and Returning"

An Introduction to the Seven Spirits Of God

Table of Contents

Preface

Matthew 23:13

Amplified translation:
But woe to you, scribes, and Pharisees, pretenders (hypocrites)! For you shut the kingdom of heaven in men's faces. For you neither enter yourselves; nor do you allow those who are about to go in to do so.

Living translation:
"Woe to you, Pharisees, and you other religious leaders, Hypocrites! For you won't let others enter the Kingdom of Heaven and won't go in yourselves."

New Mystic Translation (NMT):
"You call yourself leaders, but your fear motivation leads you no where! By your words and public actions, you don't give permission to others to enter the Kingdom of Heaven & you won't even go in yourselves."

My hope is to never shut the door to the Kingdom to anyone with or without my actions. I desire my entering the Kingdom to be an encouragement, an invitation to all.

This book is a clarion call to all to live on the other side of the veil and to experience the fullness of life.

This book is to share a few words describing my introduction to a few friends. It is not a guidebook just some stories to whet your appetite – to DARE you to believe.

It's All About Who You Know !

If you are just "curious" stop now!

Curiosity killed the cat but <u>Desire</u> will take you higher!

This book shows you away to leave normal and acquire a new set of friends.

This book is a must have if you want to know seven other creations of God, the sentient beings known as the Seven Spirits of God. In this case believe the "Hype"!
It is true and definitely true in the Kingdom of Light - "<u>it's all about who you know</u>".

Your Three Options:

(1) **READ** the book by skipping the "Introduction", "Overview", and "Conclusion" – you'll enjoy the stories in the 7 chapters or

(2) **STUDY** the entire book – you'll learn lots about a topic that may be new to you – thus making you an "informed consumer" or

(3) **BELIEVE & APPLY** the book – guaranteeing you a life unparalleled to any

Introduction

The Seven Spirits of God... you must have a hunger, a true desire if you have continued to this introduction.

> **Isaiah 11: 1-4 (AMP)**
> *¹ A shoot will come up from the stump of Jesse; from his roots a Branch will bear fruit. ² **The Spirit of the LORD** will rest on him— **the Spirit of wisdom** and **of understanding, the Spirit of counsel** and **of might, the Spirit of the knowledge and fear of the LORD**— ³ and he will delight in the fear of the LORD. He will not judge by what he sees with his eyes, or decide by what he hears with his ears; ⁴ but with righteousness he will judge the needy, with justice he will give decisions for the poor of the earth. He will strike the earth with the rod of his mouth; with the breath of his lips he will slay the wicked.*

The first 1000 times I read those verses I didn't think or believe that there were actually seven Spirits available to help. I'm still getting used to the Holy Spirit's role. Much of my Christian life, I wanted a mentor; now it seems, I have "bumped" into seven. I heard a guy mention the fact that the seven Spirits of God were available as "magistrates & tutors..." and I quickly dismissed that "ridiculous" notion until two things happened.

The 1ˢᵗ was a revelation of Hebrews 11:6 – "And without faith it is impossible to please God, because anyone who comes to him <u>must believe that He exists</u> and that he rewards those who earnestly seek him. "

| If you continue journeying, get & use a journal! |

So, in my devotional time, which I now call my "engaging with the Kingdom" time (another book) – I was getting some revelation about interacting with angels (another book) and I "realized" a principle Hebrews 11:6 was not just a great verse about us & God but **a principle of knowing all spiritual beings.** (Note: God is a Spirit, John 4). So you could read Hebrews 11:6 as:

"**And without faith it is impossible to relate to a Spirit being, because anyone who comes to a Spirit being must first believe it exists…**"

So, if you don't <u>believe</u> that the 7 Spirits of God exist then

So the 2nd thing, I was studying the topic of "adoption" and reading excerpts from a book called, "Adoption in the Roman World" by Hugh Lindsay – I read the following passage:

> "…The adoption ceremony was carried out in the <u>presence of seven witnesses</u>. Now, supposing the adopting father died, and then supposes there was some dispute about the right of the adopted son to inherit, one or more of the original <u>seven witnesses</u> stepped forward and swore that the adoption was genuine and true. Thus the right of the adopted person was guaranteed and he entered into his inheritance."

So with the combination of the spiritual and historical revelations – I began to believe the 7 Spirits existed. So that's my introduction to my "almost" introduction.

Enjoy who I found,

New Mystic

Overview

<u>Sola Scriptura</u>

Here is more scripture than I had before I met any of the seven. OK, allow scripture to interpret scripture, I was led to another truth about the seven: The biblical statement "eyes of the Lord" is actually an inference or an idiom for the Seven Spirits of God. Follow the trail below:

<u>Genesis 6:8(NKJV)</u>
> [8] *But Noah found grace in the <u>eyes of the LORD</u>.*

<u>1 Kings 15:5(NKJV)</u>
> [5] *because David did what was right in <u>the eyes of the LORD</u>, and had not turned aside from anything that He commanded him all the days of his life, except in the matter of Uriah the Hittite.*

<u>2 Chronicles 16:9(NKJV)</u>
> [9] *For <u>the eyes of the LORD</u> run to and fro throughout the whole earth, to show Himself strong on behalf of those whose heart is loyal to Him. In this you have done foolishly; therefore from now on you shall have wars."*

<u>Psalm 34:15(NKJV)</u>
> [15] *The <u>eyes of the LORD</u> are on the righteous, and His ears are open to their cry.*

<u>Proverbs 22:12(NKJV)</u>
> [12] *The <u>eyes of the LORD</u> preserve knowledge; But He overthrows the words of the faithless.*

Zechariah 4:10(NKJV)

> [10] *For who has despised the day of small things? For these seven rejoice to see the plumb line in the hand of Zerubbabel. They are the eyes of the LORD, which scan to and fro throughout the whole earth."*

1 Peter 3:12(NKJV)

> [12] *For the eyes of the LORD are on the righteous, and His ears are open to their prayers; but the face of the LORD is against those who do evil."*

Revelation 5:6(NKJV)

> [6] And I looked, and behold, in the midst of the throne and of the four living creatures, and in the midst of the elders, stood a Lamb as though it had been slain, having seven horns and seven eyes, which are the seven Spirits of God sent out into all the earth.

Read it again, "seven eyes which are the seven spirits of God" – that seems crystal clear.

Starting from Genesis and ending in Revelations, "eyes of the Lord" (aka the seven Spirits of God) have been very active. They want to be busier - training believing believers who actually believe. They have been searching the globe & time for students. I think they may have found the students but not many want to enroll. I think it is a fear of some sort – I know I feared talking to any Spirit other than the Holy Spirit. Or maybe others fear the price of admission to this "Spirit school".

The price = being willing & teachable

One part of being teachable - other than being a "believing, believer who believes" **– is the ability to focus and not be distracted.**

One Thing

Before this journey began, I had to discipline my very active mind. We live in an age of information (aka an epoch distractions). A phrase came to mind, "ONE THING I DESIRE…" and I realized it was tough for me to focus on **ONE THING** for any period time. So I thought that "meditation" might help me focus on the **ONE THING**.

So, I searched the internet for some free guidance on the "art/discipline of meditation". Note: My goal was to focus NOT empty my mind! I found lots of info but found a few steps that I could adopt and modify for me.

My modified steps:

1. **Set aside a calm, quiet place (I tried soothing music but it became another distraction)**

2. **Sit comfortably (note: when I laid down I would sleep, so sit)**

3. **Slow your breathing**

4. **Breathe deeply (slow & steady)**

5. **I would focus on an image in my mind (eyes closed): "An ocean shore, me looking down at the gentle waves lapping my feet then watching the water recede…"**

6. **I would try to set my breathing on the wave cycle: breathing in with the wave coming to shore; breathing out as the water receded**

7. **I would try to stay focused only at the water for just 5 minutes.**

It took me several weeks (actually months) before I could get to five uninterrupted minutes. It would take me 30 minutes just to get through steps 1 – 5.

My exercises were to increase or build my ability to **focus** and not be so easily distracted. I would follow the steps as often as I could. I was unaware of how beneficial this discipline was going to become in the future.

Summary of Interactions

1. **Sit** at the feet of the Spirit of Wisdom;

2. **Walk** with the Spirit of Understanding;

3. **See** (perceive) with the Spirit of Counsel;

4. **Rule** (dominate) with the Spirit of the Lord;

5. **Work** with the Spirit of Might;

6. **Live** with the Spirit of Knowledge;

7. **Stand hand-in-hand** with the Spirit of the fear of the Lord

A book could be written for each of the above points, but that is for one of you to write. My goal is an introduction.

Galatians 4:1-2 (NIV)
[1] What I am saying is that as long as an heir is underage, he is no different from a slave, although he owns the whole estate. [2] The heir is subject to guardians and trustees until the time set by his father.

I believe the "**guardians**" are: the Word & the Holy Spirit (Paraclete); while the "**trustees**" are the Seven Spirits of God.

The next chapters will expound on my first encounters. I hope to motivate you to take your own journey.

Chapter One – Spirit of Wisdom

In the September 2011, I was researching some references in some material that I was reading. The book had cited the topic of "Adoption" from the ancient Roman culture. I rarely take information at face value, so I was validating the "foundation" of the teachings that I was reading. Some findings from that research caused me to take or retake a look at my concept of seven Spirits of God versus my current understanding of seven 'natures' or seven expressions of the Holy Spirit. I was challenged but not converted.

Anyway later in the Fall on a Friday night (probably November), I called a friend and asked, "What is that chapter in the book of Proverbs that is about the Spirit of Wisdom?" He replied, "Chap. 8".

Stop and read Proverbs Chapter 8

So later that night, I was reading Proverbs 8 and fell asleep.

The next morning, I woke up to a dream. Well I think it was a dream. Anyway, I woke to this thought, *"Wisdom will leave her mark on you. Wisdom will leave her mark on you."*

It was so clear, I thought I heard it. I'm not a morning person. I had never wakened like that. The thought was so strange, *"Wisdom will leave her mark on you. Wisdom will leave her mark on you."* I assumed that my Friday night "meditation" on Proverbs 8 had truly left it's "mark on me".

Since I was up late reading Proverbs (and I am a night person). I slept through to the afternoon. The only thing on my agenda was to get to church that night. We were having a guest speaker. I had heard good things about him.

I got to church early; got my front row seat. I was not disappointed; the guest speaker shared an amazing message from book of Genesis on the life of Abraham.

After the message, the guest speaker invited folks up for prayer. I forget the specific call but being on the front row, I was the first to step forward but not the 1st to receive prayer. From my perspective, it seemed that the minister was avoiding me. He started at the beginning of the line that was closer to the wall but I was in the middle where he just finished speaking.

This was an excellent opportunity to be offended and I took full advantage of it.

I wish I could say patiently, but after about 10 minutes, I was a bit mad. I realized my negative attitude did not create a good environment for the anointing (or any good thing), so I began focusing on the Lord and trying to "get my heart right". After awhile, I stopped thinking about the time and stopped justifying my "right to be first". I peeked to my right and even more people were between us; "Ugghhh". Back to getting my heart right...

Thus, I started to utilize my meditation training.

I guess I finally got my focus off of the speaker. My imagination started creating a scene (aka a vision). Some have made visions into some super spiritual experience or a mysterious event for the elite.

Visions are available to all. Visions can be triggered by your desire that utilizes your imagination

---

So, while in the prayer line, I had a vision. In this vision:

I was outside like in a place that looked like Colorado. I was standing in this field. In the distance, I saw this "hooded figure" on a rocky mountain trail. This figure waved toward me. It seemed to be signaling to me to come up where it was. As I approached the hooded figure, a voice said, "Abraham was NOT mentored; he was NOT taught by Wisdom." I was stunned that the voice in my 'imagination' was mentioning something that related to the message earlier that evening. (I say related but definitely not from the message.) In a moment, I was standing next to the figure. The voice in my head then said, "The road through the mountains is hard, but Wisdom will be your guide. As I stood in front of the figure, somehow I knew that the figure was the Spirit of wisdom. I was not sure of the source of the voice was the figure. But the hooded figure in front of me began to say, "To travel is not by strength but by skill - skill is taught in the place called REST (I later found that "the place called REST is a real place, but it is not on earth); strength is created by facing resistance which your mind and body are very familiar with. She was definitely equipped to make me able to climb my assigned mountain. She made an emphasis, "getting strong through resistance is similar to learning from your Mistakes; but He (the one called 'mistakes') is a hard teacher; Wisdom is a good teacher)." She continued to say, Abraham learned from mistakes and not from Wisdom. As she spoke, I retained what she said but it was different from just hearing something – her words were being planted in me. (Was I being marked by Wisdom?) The thought came to me, "you are not looking like I thought you would look, the hooded brown drab monk looking outfit made her look more like a witch…" She responded to my thoughts, "If you beheld my beauty, you would lust and be distracted – so it's better for you if I appear in this form". Knowing me, I nodded in agreement. In a flash, I was back in the building – I had returned to standing in the prayer line.

I stood there pondering this encounter. I had met some of my assigned angels but this was different. I opened my eyes to see where I was and I was still in standing in the prayer line waiting. But, now he was only two people away. I'm not sure how long I was gone or how long my conversation was with the Spirit of wisdom.

But moments later, the guest minister was standing in front of me – I didn't know whether to share what I had experienced or get ready to receive. I switched to "receive" mode and the minister gave me a very relevant prophetic word. But I must say that my encounter with the Spirit of Wisdom was much better.

Proverbs 8:22-23
"The Lord formed and brought Wisdom forth at the beginning of His way, before His acts of old.

Wisdom was inaugurated and ordained from everlasting, from the beginning… and I believe she is waiting & wanting to be active in your life & mine. The Lord brought forth Wisdom at the beginning of His way. And in my vision, it seems the Lord placed Wisdom at the beginning of my way, before my acts of awe.

After that 1st encounter on that Saturday night, the next morning I got another lesson.

I woke up. Sat up in bed, looked around my (messy) room and my eyes locked on a shirt that was draped over some books. I thought, "I love that saying on my shirt, **Skilled and Dangerous**". And then she said, *"its lesson to you is: being skilled makes you*

18

*more dangerous to your opponent than being experienced".
Wisdom will teach (tutor me) in skills. Abraham was a man of
experience, not wisdom."*

So that was my weekend with Wisdom.

I really do believe she and the other Spirits do wish to engage with
every believing believer who actively believes.

Proverbs 8:17
[17] *I love those who love me, and those who seek me
early and diligently shall find me.*

As with every relationship, you must spend time cultivating it. I
think verse 17 was written on behalf of Wisdom and the other six
Spirits.

A chat between friends

I said: "Your voice is very familiar."

She said: "I have spoken to you before."

I said: "You could have told me – I assumed you were the Holy Spirit."

She said: "I am a holy Spirit."

I said: "You know what I mean; I would have thought you would have identified yourself, so I would know it was you versus some other."

She said: "We do not seek recognition, like you and your name tags; I seek your growth"

I said: "I like my name tags"

She said: "I know"

It's time to start your relationship and time for me to spend more time with her.

It's time to spend more time with our Spirit friends

Chapter Two – Spirit of Counsel

She introduced herself. She described herself - not a physical description but more about "what & how she would teach". I would say that "perspective" is her field of expertise.

It seems that the Spirit of counsel comes from a "future" perspective and not from the "now" perspective. She, the Spirit of counsel helps you navigate to your destination (aka DESTINY). She helps you define your perspective(s). Once you see or learn to consistently see from the Spirit of counsel's view and gain an "embedded" perspective. With this skill, you can then function as a King. Kings move things (resources under their command) into place. Again, the goal of all of the seven is to tutor you so that you can reign in this life as a King.

This dream shows the benefits of a relationship with the Spirit of counsel:

In this February 11, 2012 encounter, I was walking down a well lit hallway. I wasn't alone; someone was walking next to me. As we were beginning to walk past a set of double doors, my eyes were drawn to the sign above the door. The sign flashed on and off, "__COUNCIL IN SESSION__". Well obviously the sign was my motivation to continue walking, but the "person" I was with --- bumped me; yep, 'hip checked' through the double doors.

Shocked by the action and trying to gather myself, I stood ready to point the finger and defend myself. I lowered my eyes, cleared my throat, and said, "It's not my fault, I read the sign; I had no intention of entering..." I turned to identify the true source of the interruption but there was no one there. I stood alone.

I look towards the group. The members in the room turned toward my direction. To my surprise, they stood to attention. No salutes, but a definite sign of respect. Puzzled by this action, I looked around. I expected to see some dignitary, ambassador, or maybe the "person" who bumped me. I was just glad that they didn't seem to be too agitated by my interruption.

No one "yelled" at me, I looked up & around the "counsel chamber". The room's members returned to their seats around a large table. The table and the attendees seemed to be on an elevated platform. I tried to focus on who was around the table. I tried to make out their faces but for some reason I couldn't perceive any of their facial features. They all had on robes of the same color, blue. The robes reminded me of choir or judge's robes.

Since the faces were not clear, I turned my attention to the name plates. But I couldn't make out the writing either. I thought it odd that I could clearly read the sign over the double doors but now I was not able to make out facial features or the name plates. The "delegates" returned back to business.

*I wasn't escorted out; I looked for an empty seat. I walked up the few steps, sat down, reached for the name plate, and turned it toward me. I could read it - the name plate said, "**Son of God**".*

> *A thought shouted in my mind, "There's been a vacant seat at the table; it needs to be filled".*

I put the name plate down and tried to figure out what was going on in this room —"What's their business?

The table was on a platform, set up in a half-oval layout with each seat facing the center. In the center of the oval, scenes or images appeared - sort of like scenes in a big "snow globe" (but no snow or shaking). The first scene that I saw appeared; it looked like some small land mass, maybe a nation. As the image materialized, each delegate, in turn, around the table made a statement about the scene, the image. After the last delegate made his case, the image transformed – shifted to a "new topic of discussion". It seemed the business was to "talk, make declaration on whatever appeared…"

The next the image appear. It was a nicely dressed black mature female, she looked familiar but I could not recall the face. I was searching my brain – the face was so familiar - someone, some celebrity from a movie or TV show. I was so fixated; I didn't hear the comments the delegates were making.

The image change again. By this time, I had figured out the "business of the delegates" – well maybe not but I wanted to engage. So this third image seemed to be a scene of a conflict between two individuals. I raised my hand. And to be first, I *quickly blurted out my opinion, my statement. I waited to hear the next delegates' statements but there was silence, a pregnant pause - no delegate statements. To my dismay, in unison, the delegates said, "**So be it!**"*

I sat stunned. How many decisions have been made in this room, around this table without the input/influence of a son of God?

Again, as you embark on this journey of "making new friends" in the unseen realm – document **every encounter!** Every encounter is a multi-layer lesson. Every time you re-visit (and you should often) – you will change. Do not just re-read your encounters. Return to them, yes, revisit them. In the spirit realm "now is now" even if it is "later"; it is still "now".

After revisiting the above dream (not just every minute but spacing it over days, weeks, & months - I realized that my partner in the hallway was the Spirit of counsel. And she bumped me into a place that I need to be. I have a seat to fill and a responsibility.

I am sure you have places to go and seats to fill. So take a walk on the "wild-side", a see where your new friends will take you.

You to have friends in "High Places"!

Chapter Three – Spirit of Might

These chapters are not in time sequence order of the encounters. I'm actually not sure what order these chapters are in. But, I do know that meeting the Spirit of Wisdom not only was cool and amazing but it gave me faith to meet the others.

I believe "the Kingdom realm" or God's unseen domain is more real than the domain that we are in now. Well I'm learning that it is true. Movies, like "The Matrix", help our minds understand.

> **The more that we start to believe; the more we can engage with the other citizens of the king's domains.**

I have yet to see the Spirit of Might but I think he prefers that. I say "he" because I perceive his voice as masculine or maybe our interactions or the 'tone' of the interactions feel manly. He has that bodyguard feel (and yes, I know there are female body guards).

Anyway, he described his unseen self in this manner: He causes your kingly reputation to precede you (i.e. terror went before God and the Jews as was witnessed by citizens of the walled city of Jericho – **read Joshua 2: 8-11**). You feel a Shock wave before you hear the sound; He is an effective, unseen, yet perceivable Force.

I understood him to say, "The Spirit of the world is like gravity which seeks to hold you earthbound. Just as lift and thrust overcome gravity, the Spirit of Might overcomes the Spirit of the world. His function is to allow you the freedom to function- to do, to be able.

> **THE SPIRIT OF MIGHT ALLOWS US TO BE ABLE TO BE!**

During the writing, I was reminded of the time I was driving some friends back to their college. We were driving through many small towns in Kansas. We went through one town and I thought the railroad tracks were like curbs. So, I saw the sign for the next set of tracks I had my foot ready to slow down and ease over the tracks. As we went over the first set and then slowly up and over the 2nd set of tracks, I turned my head. A bright light filled my eyes and loud horn was just a bit louder than the screams of 4 guys in the car.

One second, I'm staring down a train; the next millisecond, the train is passing behind us. We kept screaming even after the train passed. It was odd how we were just a few feet away from the speeding train and my foot never left the brakes. I think the Spirit of Might was active in my life before we were introduced.

Being a son of God is ALL about BEING, not doing.

This truth is communicated in every interaction with the seven Spirits. I think it is a founding principle. According to Isaiah 11 and the recordings of His life, the Spirit of Might was upon Jesus. He gave Him "room, space, and an environment" to function. They can aid us and can help us function.

You and I have amazing potential!

Here are some scriptural examples of the Spirit of Might in action:

- **Matthew 5**
  "Seeing the crowds, He went up on the mountain..." This chapter is about the delivery of the great speech known as "The Beatitudes". I was shown that the logistics and crowd control for this and similar events (i.e. the feeding of the 5000) were actually supernatural undertakings that were successful due to the Spirit of Might. Among other things, the Spirit of Might makes events go "smoothly". He is the "man" behind the scenes.

- **Luke 4:28-30(NIV)**
  *[28] All the people in the synagogue were furious when they heard this. [29] They got up, drove him out of the town, and took him to the brow of the hill on which the town was built, in order to throw him off the cliff. [30] **But he walked right through the crowd and went on his way.***

  This was another feat of the Spirit of Might. (If I'd known about his skills, I would've recruited him to my team when I was a running back during my high school football seasons.)

- **Psalm 91:7**
  *"A **thousand** may **fall** at your side, **ten thousand** at your right hand, but it will not come near you."*

  (That's what I'm talking about! I think he must have invented the phrase "I got your back".)

The clearest picture that he showed me of how he functions was; what I call the "aerodynamic affect". It can be seen when an object is placed in a wind tunnel or in those sport car commercials – in which visible forces appear around the moving object.

He showed me that I must be moving in my destiny so that the Spirit of Might will be effective for, around, and with me

---

He also inferred that his "protection" was different than angelic protection. I'm not sure if one is more superior to the other; I assume that they would be very complimentary and work in tandem.

In the days we are living in, we need all the allies we can handle.

Teamed with the residents of the unseen, we are UNSTOPPABLE!

Two more revelatory benefits assessable with this relationship:

(1)   **Romans 8:37 (AMP)**
      "Yet amid all these things we are more than conquerors and gain a surpassing victory through Him Who **loved** us."

The 7 Spirits of God are all motivated by Love!

---

(2)   If you will take a little extra effort to wear these three *armors: "When fully armored (wearing the armor of Light [Romans 13:12], the armor of Righteousness [2 Corinthians 6:4], & the armor of Might [Ephesians 6:10]) – at least with this armor of Might – the wearer of the armor emits a frequency that renders "flaming missiles", "fiery darts" impotent – they cannot fly or penetrate into your sphere."

*If you want more information on acquiring the three armors, please contact me. The armors do NOT come with the relationships – they must be acquired.

The Spirit of Might wants to watch your back!

Chapter Four – Spirit of the Lord

2 Corinthians 3:17 (NKJV)
*[17] Now the Lord is the Spirit; and **where the Spirit of the Lord is**, there is liberty.*

I've read this verse many times. I have heard the verse a thousand times but, only in this last year did I ever read this verse with emphasis on <u>the person</u> of the *Spirit of the Lord.* It seems where He is, liberty is not far behind.

I have only heard his voice in dreams. And once I've heard him, there is usually a scene or a picture that accompanies the words I hear.

The Spirit of the Lord would have you "do as He does". He trains by you following or shadowing his actions until you make them your own. An audio/visual of this can be seen in the 1999 movie, "The Matrix". The scene where Morpheus trains Neo in the two programs: the Combat Simulation program and the Jump program.

John 3:31 (AMP)
*"**He who comes from above** (heaven) is far above all others; he who comes from the earth belongs to the earth, and talks the language of earth his words are from an earthly standpoint. He who comes from heaven **is far above all** others far superior to all others in prominence and in excellence."*

He, the Spirit of the Lord, shows how to approach your adversary from a "higher" place which gives you the advantage and your strike is deadly to the opponent.

Never come up from a low place to attack when you can come down from a high place to assure the victory.

An audio/visual of this can be seen in the 2009 movie, "Avatar" when the lead character captured the large red flying creature, the Great Leonopteryx (aka *Toruk* in the Na'vi language).

This dream was the clearest (not last) account of his interactions with me:

"In the dream, I was sitting/laying in a lounge chair in my front yard. A dog was sitting to my right. I heard a sound. I turned to see a group marching up the street, towards us. I lay back on the lounge chair. The group seemed organized, wore uniforms and helmets – an army of some type. I sat there and they continued to march past me and the dog. Their marching, their numbers, their demeanor were meant to terrorize but the dog & I were not intimidated. We looked at them; they looked at us. It seemed my "you-don't- scare-me-face" had an effect on the passing troops. They returned my looks with even more mean faces. In

response to their new looks, I pulled a sword from under the chair and laid it in my lap. This new addition caused quite a stir in the group. They seemed to pass this new information up the line and then the group stopped. With some unheard order, two from the group stepped out from the columned formation. They stood a few feet from me to my left. I looked down at my sword. I expected it to be shiny but it was speckled with small rust spots. I looked back up to the two in uniform. They started running towards my house. I grabbed the sword and chased them. They entered the house before me. I searched but I could not find the intruders. After a while, I stopped the search and stood outside frustrated. Why couldn't I find the two? Why did they go into the house? Where did they go? What is going on? And why was my sword rusty? I stood pondering & wondering; standing fatigued and in a state of despair. I felt defeated. Then, I sensed something – I think it was audible – I heard the words, "**Start the dream over**". I paused. I heard it again, "**Start the dream over**". I then remembered hearing a testimony about "stepping back into a dream" or "returning to a vision" – but I had never experienced anything like that. Ordinarily it is at this point in my experiences, I begin to reason through the possible options and outcomes – I analyze the what-ifs – which usually led to "paralysis by analysis". Unusual for me, **I heeded the advice of the voice (I now believe the voice, my aid, my tutor was the Spirit of the Lord)** – I went back to the beginning of the dream.

So again, I was back sitting/laying on my lounge chair. And again here came the troops. The interaction between troops & I began again. And again, I laid the sword on my leg. But this time, when the two stepped out from their ranks – I jumped up and stood in front of them. With one fluid sweeping motion, I raised my rusty blade and removed their heads from their uniformed bodies. Yes, the thrill of victory! I stood feeling very pleased with the decision to return to the dream: in this version there was no chasing; no intruders in my house; no loosing intruders in my house; no fatigue; no despair; no frustration... The thrill was short lived – the thrill melted into an odd feeling, a strange feeling. If I was a comic book hero, I'd say it was a "spidey sense". I looked around and the rest of the troops were still standing there. Hmmmm, the voice was right earlier...

So, I went back to the beginning of the dream (again, again). I'm in the lounge chair lying down and the dog is sitting to my right. So far "man's best friend" has only been watching me, no barking, and only holding down his patch of grass.) I hear a sound; I see the marching troops coming my way. This time before they got close to me, <u>I arise from the resting place.</u> I turned and faced the approaching enemy. This time there was no doubt in my mind that this group was the enemy and they had very hostile intentions, sent to occupy my territory. I looked for my sword, my rusty, spotted sword. I reached for it, but my right hand & forearm transformed into a blade. It looked as if there was a sword blade attached to my elbow. Wow! I wasn't expecting that. I went to touch my new blade with my left hand but my left arm had changed too. Both blades were shiny, no rust in sight. In the face of my enemy, I had been transformed. I ran towards the enemy with both arms extended. I slew the entire group. I was a bit winded but very, very pleased – my foes vanquished! But that "strange feeling" came back. I realized there were probably more troops than *just the ones on my street. Could this be an invasion? Well, the voice has a good track record…*

So, I went back to the beginning (again, again, again). I'm lying in lounge chair enjoying the sun on my face – this rest is good. But, my peace is disturbed. Somehow I know that something foreign has entered my atmosphere, my domain, my realm of authority. I stand. I look to my left. I look to my right. I see in the distance something in the sky. It looks like, I don't know… but at this distance – I can't see a plane or parachutes. I start walking towards the sight. It becomes clearer – there is a "black hole in the sky". These uniformed beings are dropping out of this hole. I've never seen anything like this. They were just falling to earth and landing on their feet. After they landed, they would quickly join other groups or squads. The enemy was gathering, organizing, and preparing. As I stood looking at their growing numbers; I began to grow. In seconds, I was as tall and massive as a mountain. With my now colossal hands, I reached for this hole in the sky. I crushed it. And said, "No More Entry, this GATE is Closed!" I raised my legs and began to trample the enemy under my size X feet. This felt like being MORE THAN A CONQUEROR! It felt very, very, very good."

The Spirit of the Lord will teach & demonstrate Kingdom Standards! This is one standard: **Ne Humanus crede** - "Trust no human". Everyone who has been resurrected with Jesus is a new creature, no longer "mere human".

We need to know who we are and who we are not.

The following verses will help you change and build your paradigm:

- John 5:34; John 7:46; John 10:32-35

I did receive this other guidance after I was seeking some insight to an encounter. I've learned that I can ask questions of the seven and get answers. Just like any other relationship you may have with people who may know more than you or have unique experiences. Anyway, I heard this from the Spirit of the Lord:

> *"When a foe sees you dressed in the armor of Righteousness, they see the One who holds them together (their creator & ultimate destroyer). Demons, our foes, will not risk a confrontation and thus losing their little time they have left in this domain. Thus, you may not be challenged by adversaries of this level."*

A week or so after, I heard the above. I found (or was led) to this scripture:

Luke 8:27-28 (NKJV)
[27] And when He stepped out on the land, there met Him a certain man from the city who had demons for a long time. And he wore no clothes, nor did he live in a house but in the tombs.

[28] When he saw Jesus, he cried out, fell down before Him, and with a loud voice said, "What have I to do with You, Jesus, Son of the Most High God? I beg You, do not torment me!"

It was nice to have a supporting scripture, but I'm learning to trust Him in our relationship.

Like in all relationships, you can build on each interaction. The more the interactions, the more the opportunities to bond, to befriend, to trust, to relate, to get to know each other.

So get started, you need to hear what he has to say.

Freedom is available to all who hear and are willing to act on the voice of true friends.

Chapter Five – Spirit of Knowledge

I'm learning that 'true belief' or 'really believing' allows a person, any person to do the extra ordinary.

During a discussion with the Spirit of wisdom, we discussed the topic of Rest that is referenced in the book of Hebrews. From that interaction, I learned that there is an actual place called Rest.

I would think about this place, read Hebrews chapter four, meditate on this "…Sabbath rest that remains for the people of God".   During a time of meditating on this chapter, I went to this place called, Rest. I would periodically return. I believe in this place all seven Spirits congregate. It reminded me of a high school "Teachers Lounge" but in this place students were welcomed.

By this time I had met several of the Spirits of God but I desired to meet them all.

Desire is a key

I was not sure of the protocol, but this time when I returned to this place called Rest. I said. Who's next? I believe, I saw someone step forward. I heard,

> *"Time is a place, it is a room that you can enter and has three sides. One side has a door that leads to the past, another side has a door that leads to the present, and the other side has a door that leads to future. If you enter the room, you can experience all three phases of time - all at once via your spirit. It will help if you experience this room from your spirit and not your soul.*
>
> *You regularly view knowledge from the vantage of your soul. Knowledge is thus, time stamped. You are*

comfortable with time but, time is a temporal attribute not an eternal attribute. You must learn to experience multiple events that occur simultaneously in the NOW and not time based in a soul sequence. This soul sequence is a physical law not a spirit being law, constraint. "

There are laws in the spirit realms that you can learn and operate

Truth abides in the realms of the Father. This truth is valuable and useful in all realms. There is something about what "I think I know" and what "I need to know". I believe the Spirit of Knowledge is busy dividing the two and training us to live with the true truth.

During a time of engaging with the Father, I saw this scene:

"My brain was being fed into a large shredder. The shredder was powered on and my shredded brain produced 3 large bags. Each bag had large letters on them: **K-N-O-W-L-E-D-G-E**.

I then saw three angels – each one picked up a bag and proceeded to drop them into a roaring fire. As I watched the bags burn, I became angry. I thought what a waste – all that I had acquired from self study and from a year at a Bible school – all being destroyed."

I came out of the vision, but I was still stunned; actually offended. It seemed that my 'vast' knowledge was not as valuable as I thought. Can knowledge depreciate?

The Spirit of knowledge was trying to convey to me:

1. Knowledge is not as valuable as revelation;

2. Your soul acquired information (knowledge) has the ability to devalue and even devalue spirit provide information (revelation);

3. Now with the knowledge out of the way, you have more space for revelation.

The Spirit of Knowledge is more than a consultant. He is a tutor leading us to maturity but we must follow and accept the responsibilities of our identity.

Listen to your Tutor(s)

Chapter Six – Spirit of Understanding

Proverbs 3:5 (NIV)
*⁵ Trust in the Lᴏʀᴅ with all your heart
and lean not on your own understanding;*

As I prepared to write this chapter, the above scripture came to mind. There seemed to be emphasis on: "… not on your own understanding". Then the thought came, "He has understanding for us to lean on; His understanding is available". That understanding is actually one of His creations, a sentient being called the Spirit of understanding.

I'm learning:

1. When the door to revelation opens the corresponding change of atmosphere allows the Spirit of understanding the opportunity to train me.
2. Training happens and it occurs best within relationship and in that atmosphere

Psalm 119:130(AMP)
"¹³⁰ The entrance and unfolding of Your words give light; their unfolding gives understanding (discernment and comprehension) to the simple."

The open door is "the entrance" (opening, literally the door (gate), entrance way). He opens the door and we have the option to enter into the relationship with understanding.

The Spirit of understanding appeared to me looking very much like the Spirit of wisdom, maybe a little shorter. She wore a similar hooded, monk robe. There seemed to be a soft yellow glow that poured from the openings of her outfit. I could not make out body structure or facial features. The voice sounded feminine. She said, "*Walk with me*". As we walked, the scenery faded and it looked like I was standing in the center of an orange. Yes, I was seeing the inside of an orange. She was no longer standing next to me but I heard her voice say, "I will show you everything from the inside out".

The Spirit of understanding provides "in-sight"

She reports what one could perceive from an "internal" perspective (literally from the inside). She allows you to process 'stuff' as a whole and not dissected separate pieces. She says, "*Truth or perception is tied to context. The context is your angle of view*". She provides context, the other angles of view so that one can view the 'whole of the matter'. We need the whole of the matter to fully experience, to fully enjoy the journey.

You may be wondering why she selected an orange. That is a great question! You should ask her when you meet her. I was amazed she said, "Walk with me".

So, the inside of an orange is pretty cool but not as cool as the things you will see on your journey.

Walk with the Spirit of Understanding & you will never go astray

---

Chapter Seven – Spirit of the Fear of the Lord

Isaiah 11:3 (NIV)
³ and he will <u>delight in the fear of the LORD</u>. He will not judge by what he sees with his eyes, or decide by what he hears with his ears;

I must be honest; I was not looking forward to meeting the Spirit of the fear of the Lord. Throughout the year as I was sharing some of my encounters with friends, they would ask when I was going to meet the Spirit of the fear of the Lord. I told them that meetings were not up to me. But secretly, I was afraid. Fear is a spirit. You should have an adversarial relationship with fear. You may have spent time with Fear but, Fear is not your friend. If you have a fear of something (i.e. a fear of flying), you have been listening to and learning from that spirit. I propose you end that relationship.

Every relationship affects every other relationship

Fear will keep you from meeting new friends and will ruin existing relationships. This may have been why meeting this Spirit was so long in the making. Or the Lord was saving the best for last?

I finally confessed my fear to a friend.

In the early hours of 18 November 2011 in the Bronx, NY, I had my 1ˢᵗ encounter with the Spirit of the Fear of the Lord. I encountered him last. He was last because of my inward "fear of the unknown" actually it was an "assumed fear" based upon his name. But my desire overcame my fear and the encounter transpired anyway. Now I think, I just needed to let down my guard, my-self defenses. Fatigue has a way of doing that. The encounter happened after a long drive from Virginia to New York. I was tired from the drive (exhausted) but still trying to actively participate in an all night worship event being hosted in a Bronx church. We arrived around 10pm but my encounter happened around 2am. Most of the group that had driven into NYC was now sleeping in the basement. I remained upstairs worshipping or was I dreaming about worshipping.

The hard, uncomfortable, small pews did their best to keep me awake. *Anyway, I heard a voice say:*

> *"It's really a wrong name".   I didn't understand that. Then I heard, "I deal with all the lovers in your life. Those false lovers actually FEAR the true Lover of your soul!*

> *"Because you have joined with so many other lovers – you have in the same manner "miss-labeled" me. I am actually the Lover of our soul. I ruthlessly deal with those false lovers! They have communicated a lie and have transferred their fear (and name calling) to you. Thus, you and others have wrongly called me the Spirit of the Fear of the Lord.*

> *I, the Lover of your souls am bold, even audacious! I have witnessed every adulterous encounter. I have been present at every wayward thought. He said, "He was present when Samson was "sleeping" with the whore. (I had that month been meditating on Judges 16)*

Judges 16:1, 3
> *"And Samson goeth to Gaza, and seeth there a woman, a harlot, and goeth in unto her;*
> *³ And Samson lieth down till the middle of the night, and riseth in the middle of the night, and layeth hold on the doors of the gate of the city, and on the two side posts, and removeth them with the bar, and putteth on his*

shoulders, and taketh them up unto the top of the hill, which [is] on the front of Hebron."

I have learned that He, the lover of your soul, is not often seen because many never want to see Him.

He is a Jealous Lover

Once you relate to Him and stay relating, the other false lovers will keep their distance! Like garlic repels vampires, His fragrance on your life will repel seducers & false lovers!

He is actually very visible but we are very distracted. He is judged by his activity – he can separate you from "things" that have your heart, your attention, and your devotion.

Unlike us, he does NOT reason with his foes (false lovers); He slices and separates. Many "fear" being separated from their sources that brought them comfort, pleasure, and a pseudo-security.

If you partner with the Lover of your soul, the Father will always be the only one in your heart and your heart will be secure.

**No longer call him the Spirit of the fear of the Lord –
HE IS THE LOVER OF YOUR SOUL**

Conclusion

My family and I lived in England for almost two years. Other than the privilege of driving on the wrong side of their roads, I also had the privilege of having a British banking account. But these privileges were not easy to come about. You see in my case, I found that the UK bankers needed a personal introduction before a stranger could open an account in their bank. In their culture, it's all about relationships.

Relationships are vital in His Kingdom too. Your relationships with the individual seven Spirits of God will definitely give you something to talk about but more importantly they will assist you in this journey called life.

I've learned that Jesus knew the Lover of His soul (the Spirit of the fear of the Lord). Since, Jesus delight was in the "fear of the Lord"; he was not distracted or seduced by anything. I believe because of His relationships with the seven Spirits of God, He successfully completed His earth journey.

> **Isaiah 11: 1-3**
> *¹ A shoot will come up from the stump of Jesse; from his roots a Branch will bear fruit. ² The Spirit of the LORD will rest on him— the Spirit of wisdom and of understanding, the Spirit of counsel and of might, the Spirit of the knowledge and fear of the LORD— ³ and he will delight in the fear of the LORD. He will not judge by what he sees with his eyes, or decide by what he hears with his ears;*

Your relationship with the Seven Spirits will help you mature from being a [Greek] *"teknon"* (a spiritual baby who thinks Jesus is white and created Christianity) to being a [Greek] *"huios"* (a mature son of God who does the works of the Father, works with the Father, and enjoys setting creation free.)

That's right this book is the red pill!

Remember, this is only an introduction –
You can take your relationships as deep as you desire!

So don't just scratch the surface.

Go make some new friends; they are waiting for you!

(I still wish they would wear name tags because it would be easier to write about them.)

*The spirit of Might is like the force of wind that allows you to lean over the edge.

Please send Your Comments or stories from your journeys to me:
royalfreedom33@yahoo.com

Or

Contact me on FaceBook under the name:
New Mystic